KISSES

For Susan + Linda,
Best,

The Miami University Press Poetry Series
General Editor: James Reiss

The Bridge of Sighs, Steve Orlen
People Live, They Have Lives, Hugh Seidman
This Perfect Life, Kate Knapp Johnson
The Dirt, Nance Van Winckel
Moon Go Away, I Don't Love You No More, Jim Simmerman
Selected Poems: 1965-1995, Hugh Seidman
Neither World, Ralph Angel
Now, Judith Baumel
Long Distance, Aleda Shirley
What Wind Will Do, Debra Bruce
Kisses, Steve Orlen

KISSES

A collection of poems
by
Steve Orlen

Miami University Press
Oxford, Ohio

Library of Congress Cataloging-in-Publication Data

Orlen. Steve
Kisses : poems / by Steve Orlen
p.   cm.
ISBN 1-881163-20-2 (cloth). — ISBN 1-881163-21-0 (paper)
PS3565.R577K5 1997
811'.54 — dc21   97 - 12987
CIP

The paper in this book meets the guidelines
for permanence and durability of the Committee
on Production Guidelines for Book Longevity
of the Council on Library Resources. ∞

Printed in the U.S.A.

9 8 7 6 5 4 3 2 1

For Gail & for Cozi, for Marian Marcus & Paul Portje,
& for my parents, Milton & Florence Orlen

ACKNOWLEDGMENTS

Agni: "Authority," "Mr. & Mrs. Death"

The Atlantic Monthly: "Imagination"

The Gettysburg Review: "Nobody's Jew," "Ode: 1948"

The Kenyon Review: "God's Mistakes," "Elegy for Steve Ferreira"

Many Mountains Moving: "Confession," "I Want to be a Girl," "Genealogy"

The New England Review: "Shyness"

Ploughshares: "Poem Against Ideas"

Red Rock Review: "The Man in the Black Tuxedo," "Stolen Kisses," "Unspeakable Things"

The Southern Review: "Field Guide," " Elephant Dance"

TriQuarterly: "The Shaping Ground"

The Yale Review: "The Meaning of Romance"

Fever Dreams: Contemporary Arizona Poets (edited by Leilani Wright & James V. Cervantes, University of Arizona Press): "The Life Stories of Undistinguished Americans," "Mr. & Mrs. Death"

Outsiders (edited by Laure-Anne Bosselaar, Milkweed Editions): "Androgyny"

Thanks also to Michael Collier, Tony Hoagland, Boyer Rickel, Ellen Bryant Voigt, and Gibb Windahl, for their help with these poems. For their friendship and support, my thanks to Tina Feingold, Mike Mayo, Nancy Pitt, and Bill Van Every.

"I have heard that Balzac. . . one day found himself before a fine painting representing winter, a quiet melancholy landscape, heavy with hoarfrost, with huts here and there, and sickly peasants. After having contemplated a small house out of which meager smoke ascended, he exclaimed: 'How beautiful it is! But what do they do in that hut? What do they think about, what are their worries? Did they have a good harvest? Certainly they have payments coming due?' "

   –Baudelaire

CONTENTS

KISSES

POEM AGAINST IDEAS

I read in a book that in the Kishinev pogrom
Forty-seven Jews had been killed
But elsewhere I had read
That forty-eight Jews had been murdered
By fire, by stoning, by rifle, knife and strangling.

And I wondered if the author had accidentally left out
My Great-Uncle Emphraim Belkin, perhaps because
He was passing through, a boy, about ten years old
I was told by my aunt, and somebody had thrown
A rock at his head as he stood in a bread line.

They were starving, a family of eleven. They had fled
Odessa, and though I don't remember my geography
They must have been headed west and south
By foot towards Egypt, which was next to the Promised Land.

In Egypt, there's a family story about a camel and a bride.
And years later, in America, one sister
Would become a Communist, let her hair
Grow long, join the Polar Bear Club at Far Rockaway.
She would smoke those foul-smelling Turkish cigarettes.

One afternoon, a cornice from the roof would fall down
And crush the head of her only daughter, four years old.
Similarly, a woman wrote a book
Called *One By One By One*, referring to the deaths
Of Jews in the Holocaust, meaning to remind us

That this is the only way to think about
The deaths of so many. The book begins with stories
Of a particular group of survivors revisiting
Their home town in Germany fifty years after the war,

Calling on old neighbors, Herr Schmidt and Frau Hamberger,
The graveyard with its misplaced, upended stones,
The Jewish School now a Cultural Center.
Some of them even "felt more German," a paradox
I can barely understand.

They were quite moving, these stories, quirky,
As individual stories usually are,
But the rest of the book, which I didn't finish,
Is an intellectual history and less personal.

I told my son (who had asked) that an intellectual
Is a person who thinks a lot, and then
Thinks about what he thought about, and so on,

Until all experience, all emotions, all relationships,
All stories, can be reduced to single words:
Morality, Myth, Paradox, Guilt, and so on.
Then what good is an idea? he asked. It was an idea

About the International Jewish Banking Conspiracy
That got Hitler moving
Toward the Final Solution, and certain ideas

Are right now moving the various
Local Militia to take action against Blacks, Browns,
Asians, Jews, and Homosexuals. It was an idea

That got Marx going, and Einstein, and look
What happened there. Even Democracy, that grand
Ongoing experiment, was another bad idea
That gained currency because some good men
Took it in their heads to write a document
We could argue about for a millennium.

I remember once getting punched in the mouth
In seventh grade and I will never forget it.

And I once had an idea about the essential differences
Between men and women, between my wife
And me, between my wife and all women,
But I've since forgotten it. Today a woman told me

My use of the term "son of a bitch"
Was demeaning to women. Behind her, in the bushes,
Was a good idea all tangled up.

There are many petty people in the world.
Just look around you. Their ideas
May be right-sounding as the Ten Commandments
God gave to Moses on the Mountain,
As seductive as the Risen Christ,
As rational as Fascism, as elegant as $E=MC^2$.

But I'd rather be punched in the mouth
Because I'd tried my hardest to take that boy's
Girlfriend away from him. I succeeded,
And landed in the hedges, while she stood by,

Trembling, not knowing what to say or do. I suppose
She felt ambivalent, but that, too,
Is a story shrunk to a word.

I had a Great-Uncle named Ephraim
Who undertook a long walk from Odessa to Egypt.
He was just a boy. I can't imagine much about him

Except he was the same age my son is now. He was probably
Silly, like my son, he probably liked sweets,
He probably thought girls were put here by mistake
And probably his feet were sore.

He was a good Jew, and he probably thought
God would rescue him and his whole family
From the mess his little world was in.
He probably thought Government was a bad idea

Because it was the government that was murdering
His people. Someone, probably a man
With a bad idea planted in his brain,
Bent over in the rain – I know it was raining –
And picked up a rock and threw it.

What marked the boy as a Jew?
Maybe he had a nose like mine, maybe
He wore a funny hat and had those curly

Little sidelocks that seem to sprout
From each ear like tassels from corn. The stone
Struck his temple. The boy fell down,

My Great-Uncle Ephraim, on the wet pavement.
Maybe he was dead before he hit the ground.

The Talmud tells us that the Biblical injunction
We call "an eye for an eye, a tooth for a tooth,"
Is not to be practiced by Jews. The Talmud tells us

If we save one life we save a thousand lives,
And if we take one life
We take a thousand lives, an idea I can grasp.

I have a few friends who think, as they say,
Conceptually. They don't tell stories.

They sit around a room and argue. Each
Has an idea, which gets tossed around
Like a hot potato from person to person.

When they talk like that
My attention wanders, and I feel dumb.

But if one of them leaned across the table
Right now and slugged me for disagreeing with him,
Which I hope he won't, and he knows who he is,
I'd remember that forever. Right here, in the mouth,

So that my upper lip smashed against my eye tooth,
And I'd continue loving him.

A boy named Quegariello, who was in love,
Did just that. He's a story in my mind, a face
Suffused with blood, a quick sucker punch,

And then the stiff green hedges
Holding up my body.
He was righteous, so I didn't hit him back.

No idea could displace him, and all my poems
Are dedicated to him, and to my Great-Uncle
Ephraim, who's only a name and a scrap of story

Told me by my aunt, a boy my boy's age
Who died in the rain in a bread line in Kishinev.
As I recall, the year was 1903.

My friend is still talking in the parlor
Under an overhanging lamp that illuminates us all. The key words
Are *binomial* and *paradox*. He wants us all to give up
Thinking one way and start thinking another.

And while he is talking I confess I want
To stroke the wonderfully bony ankle and high arch
Of the woman sitting next to me. She is wearing
A gold ring on one toe, which is linked
To a gold ring on another toe. As she fidgets
The metal catches and reflects the light.

NOBODY'S JEW

The chef of the restaurant was a big bluff man
Who looked like some palooka from the comics.
In the kitchen, among the chowders and the steaks,
He'd pump out his brave stories and take
The giant, spiny, twelve-pound, old man lobster
Dripping from its tank and wave it like an obscene flag
In someone's passing face. He abused the cooks
And waiters equally, but one cook in particular,
The apprentice saucier, he humiliated the most,
For some reason I couldn't quite yet get,
Going for whatever jugular throbbed that moment
In the kitchen culture. I don't know how the saucier
Knew I was Jewish, like him,
But one night in the larder he confided
That the chef despised the Jews.
So watch your step.
I can still feel him breathing in my face
And speaking out his awful, personal, historical truths
About "our exile," "our pogroms," "our Holocaust,"
And as the summer passed he tried
In various ways without success
To enlist me in the ancient wars
Between the gentiles and the Jews.

The problem was, I couldn't stand him.
Bookish, smug, overly alert to nuances
Everyone else let pass, his face kept
That sour look of the willfully dispossessed,
Like those immigrants my uncles chuckled at,
With their sidelocks, their prayer books

21

And yarmulkes, their passive, bearded,
Ghetto insistence on being kept a race apart.
And though I thought of myself
As just another American working class kid

Who wanted to write poetry like the immortal Yeats,
What he said nagged at me, and wouldn't let me go.
So that night in the kitchen when the chef
Yelled something to the saucier, something like
Hey, Jewboy! Come taste the soup!
And the silence in its wake was like
Thick grease and the humid odors
Of the kitchen itself, whatever gorge there was in me
Rose, and as I tasted it
It yelled, *Watch your mouth!*
The chef was a coward and he made a joke.

But in that moment I hated the saucier, not the chef.
I hated his big potato nose and his chummy
Confiding sneers and the loneliness he hoarded
Like so much aging cheese
He finally got to share.
I hated him the way one hates one's self,
The way one hates one's family
In one's self, those little tics of character
Consigned to genes that rise to the ceiling

In the dark and blind you
So you can't sleep, incessant shrugs, and bickering,
The constant emotional deals we made
From room to room, from house to house,
A block, a neighborhood, an encysted,
Noisy, inventive tribal nation of us.
We roamed the earth, despised. I hated all of it.

How could we have survived! Einstein, Freud,
And all the private, melancholic shlumps,
My uncles, my father, my brother. . . .

I'm just a guy like anybody else, was all
I could think of to say, later, to the saucier,
At my station, as I let my indifferent gaze
Fall equally on customers, on silverware and plates.
And the next day, when I got fired,
I said it again, *I'm just a guy like anybody else,*

In that spoken, American, fudged pentameter
I was trying to steal from Yeats, himself among
The haters of the Jews, and saw myself as far
From the human race as that great dumb Golem
Of a lobster crawling the mucky bottom on display.
I wanted to raise it from its briny stew
And shake it in his face, and say,
I'm not your Jew. I'm nobody's Jew.

FIELD GUIDE

The afternoon is cloudy and Parisian.
Out-of-season flowers and a vagrant green.
Odors of perfume, rotten, deciduous, and blithe.

Along the street of prostitutes in the 10th arrondisement
Breasts cram high against bustiers.
Wide-mesh stockings so the chill enters
And goes out without a thank-you or goodbye.

And home-made hats, one with speckled feathers
Like a yellow-on-blue jungle bird
Who has decided not to fly but to seem to fly.

I can't know what he sees while walking,
My ten-year old, looking up and looking down,
But I see his interest quickened by
These ladies leaning in the alcoves whispering
Their blunt, early afternoon seductions:

Mon cher. Mon cher. Mon cher.

As we pass, each opens up like a daffodil
Convinced it's always Spring, and smiles
At him, unhappy hat in hand:
Maybe another place, another time.

Will you take this boy, I want to ask,
As your lawful wedded child to guide
Past the thickets and the knives?

Then let him go, down there
Where the neon flares, sputters, and goes out?

He gapes like a turkey in an open field
At the double barrels of a hunter's gun:
What does he see? What does he seem to see?

Are they his mother and my wife
At her most valentine sublime,
All breasts, nipples, waist, ass,
Red, steaming flesh blooming from the bath
To the towel's welcoming arms?

Does he imagine standing in as happy substitute
For his father in the bedroom of his mother?

Or does he see himself heading upstairs
Stripped to his underwear
To play with their *whoop-whoop*

Trucks and trains? Or like that shy
Swain he points out over there,
Snagged like a panting fish
On the hook of offered flesh?

Who stumbles now, stutters, reaches for his wallet
And finds sufficient paper of the realm
To do his business. Oh, off they stroll,
Arm in arm, *Jean et Jeannette,*

On a lunch-hour holiday of the flesh
Or of the spirit, and we are left
With the fine and sparkling baubles of our imaginations

Like the aftermath of strong, cheap wine.
Change, unspent, jingles in our pockets
And clouds like body parts drift across the sky.

ELEPHANT DANCE

Tonight, late night, my son, age eleven,
Gets up naked from his bed
And paces around the house,
Griping for his lack of sleep.
He's just a kid, his skin is smooth and sleek
As a seal pup's floating on a sheet of ice,
Although his voice, when he registers
His mild, insomniac complaint, and begs me
To read to him his adventure novel
A few minutes longer, his voice cracks,
As if some strong emotion, some dream-grief
Or dream-surprise has taken over his throat
And conducted a sliding scale of sound
From elation down to madness, and now
He can't stand still, he shifts his feet,
Doing the heavy elephant dance,
He scratches at some itch on his back
He can't quite reach, a corner of his hip, his groin,
So I look down, I can't help myself but stare
The way a man might stare at other men
In the changing room at the beach,
And there it is, his genitalia, his equipment,
A grown man's cock and balls
Swollen by dream, erect, and stipulating,
Like a snake about to strike
Some lesser creature in the trees,
Like a flagpole those minor mountaineers
Stuck in the snow to say, "Kilroy was here,
Kilroy has conquered."
Why haven't I noticed it before?

It is surrounded by a thin halo of hair
So I think of angels, those half-human messengers
Ascending and descending, faltering,
As heartened or disheartened
As the light that guides them,
They can't make up their minds between
The heavens above and the earth below
Where my son stands, half-asleep
And half-awake, a boy, a man,
Until, bored by this nothing-to-do,
He kisses me lightly on the cheek
Then lugs his new body to its old bed.

SHYNESS

I had a girlfriend once for several years
And though I loved her in those ways
Teenagers can be said to love
The problem was, she rarely spoke.
By this I mean the common, everyday
Passages of speech between two kids
Walking home from school or in the back seat,
What rises after
Shouldn't we stop? or *Want a cigarette?*

It got so I would glance above her head
For one of those balloons
Flooded with the simplest words for how she felt.
And for a while I actually believed
Her silences composed an exquisite code
Indecipherable but possible to feel, and insufficient
To the yearning of a teenage boy
In love, unbearable, carried home, to bed.

Imagine, at the dance, leaning close,
That lovesick lipstick smell, her breasts, our sweat,
Then silence starting to invade, now
A mouse of irritation, now a heavy bear
Of sullenness, now the fox's face of doubt –
Am I not worth it, after all,
This girl's incredible, unspoken
Loving attention like a laser that could burn
Away the tender muscles of the heart?

"Say *something*," I would say, again, and again,
Until I wanted to smash her like a doll
That wouldn't cry when squeezed. And the hours necking,
And her beauty itself, extraordinary,
A cheerleader and a prom queen, far better
Than I deserved, solved none of this
Intractable strangling in her throat,
The effort, the blushing, the sweetest shy sister
Of the family, until that summer

The family decided it wasn't nature
But pathology, and sent her to a therapist
Who hit on the solution: *Sodium amytal methedraline.*
Truth serum. I would pick her up afterwards,
And she would step into my car, and with the chemical
Dilating her veins, she would talk,
Oh, talk. Amazing: first, that buzzing nothing,
Then the door would open for a moment, for a word,
Then one more, and out they would parade

Like a dazed family for its photograph:
I need   I care   I love   I worry   I can't
Then we would make a few decisions, whether
Pizza or a drive, and if a drive, where to pull over,
On this shaded, unlit street, or that,
And then the talking, a motor
On a small assembly line, would hesitate,
Miss a gear, slow down, stop.
It was as though the distances between

One stubborn *No* and the next got closer,
Got swollen like a toothache, so all that was left
Was to lean even closer in the back seat
And seal her mouth with mine, twist her tongue in mine,

Her breasts, my hands, until she gave in –
Once, that very once, and never again –
Until we shuddered in release as good
As anything, as good or better than speech,
For a while, a few moments, then the silences again.

ELEGY FOR STEVE FERRIERA

What a fascinating, complicated thing it was to watch:
A drop of water in a spoon, flare of match,
A little hiss of boiling water,
The shredded snag of cotton, all so delicate,

The habitual hand reaching for
The habituated, gloriously expectant map of flesh. . .

Find the vagrant vein, slide the needle in,
Push the plunger a small bit, draw blood,
Then push the plunger all the way and wait
For the reward: pain, and relief from pain,
And then an extra jolt.

Like getting hit by a sudden truck?
Or like the longest orgasm that would ever
Electrify the flesh? Or like the blinding light
The ecstatics saw in the inner eye in the dark?

I'll never know, though afterwards
There was always in my friend
That soft grin of pleasure, and drool,
An infant at the breast.

Then his eyes would seem as if a thin
Transparent shade had been pulled down.

Wasn't there one of them you knew
In junior high, the boy you envied
For the way his entrance into class

Struck terror in the teacher? And wasn't there always
Something sweet melting on his tongue?

And did you stand beside him, trembling,
When he got his first tattoo? Or watch,
From the doorway, when he got his first blow job
From the smartest girl in eighth grade class?

And didn't his killer say, in the newspaper,
That he'd asked for it – *Go ahead, shoot*, he said –
And didn't he run a full two blocks
Down the alley before he died?

I would like here to remember my friend
Who always wanted more, and died from it.

At four or five already a future bad boy,
He would slide under the fence that fenced us in,
And turn from the other side, and face me, grinning:
The boy inside and the boy outside
Like warpings in an everlasting mirror.

THE LIFE STORIES OF
UNDISTINGUISHED AMERICANS
(1900–1920)

for Reg Gibbons

In the book of undistinguished American men
And women, those without significant event nonetheless
Have oddities that distinguish them one from the other,
The Polish Sweat Shop Girl and *The Igorrote Brave,*
The Farmer's Wife and *The Autodidact.*
How many lives there've been!

Of course, they're all dead by now,
Similar markers on similar graves.
So you, now, when a man or woman
Emerges from the crowd and tugs at your sleeve,
And says, *My life would make a novel!*
Perhaps you'll listen, asking where they're from
And what they've done, and perhaps you'll nod,
And jot it down, and say *Amen.*

What else is left at the end of a life?
We all know it: a few favorite knickknacks,
Shoes too big or too small, a chain of keys
To God knows what unopened doors –
All tossed in the trash by the undertaker's wife.

And then the secrets no one else would possess
But the dead themselves –
Those uncollected frenzied passing moments –
Those, too, gone. So God bless

The author of this book, Mr. Hamilton Holt,
Who preserved, in print, the lives of these
Undistinguished American men and women,
The Japanese Servant, The Irish Cook,
The Itinerant Minister, The Italian Boot Black,
Not a hero to be counted, neither king nor queen,
Nor murderer nor savior, only the little ones
Crouched at the bottom of the list.

Did I ever tell you the time I pissed with a star?
I'd been eating in a fancy New York restaurant
And went downstairs to the bathroom,
One of those dingy, stinky, cramped
Tiny rooms with a toilet and a grimy sink,
And as I was shaking myself off, the door
Swung open and there he was, the man with the mouth,

The man with the tongue who taught us how
To sass and sing, the great star, Mick Jagger.
And he said to me, "Hey, mate!" And I said
Back to him, "Hey, mate!" God bless that moment.
Thank God for the extraordinary to show me my place.
In that tiny room, his light shone out.
In that little space, we were at last ourselves,
The Man Who Pissed with Mick Jagger
And *The Man Who Pissed with Steve Orlen,*
And lucky for me, and lucky for him!

ODE: 1948

I don't remember where I stood because that house
Is gone now, and with it those beautiful women,
Nor what I might have felt except the pleasures
I took those Saturday nights my mother and my aunts
Danced back and forth
Like lights across a darkened field
Between the bedroom and the bath;
Nor why they let me watch as they got dressed,
As their body parts would wiggle, twist, tighten,
And fill out their underpants, their girdles
And bras in ways you can't imagine anymore.

Which is why I wish you could have stood there
With me for the complications of the garter belts,
The sheer, transparent, flesh-colored nylon stockings
Unrolled slowly up one leg and then the other
And heard the faint whisper of electric power
Coursing through a line; and beheld the dresses,
Shorter now, more blatantly colorful because the war
Was finally over, and then the jewels, fingered
For their gold and silver clinks, then the unstoppered
Odor of Chanel dabbed on earlobes, neck and wrist.

When one aunt, and then another, would open wide
Her mouth before the mirror, then do, like this,
In one swift motion, apply the thick cake of color
Like sherbet to her lips, could they have known
They got a small boy drunk? *Don't go!*
I'd call out, but they're gone, each of them,
Just as Bette Grable is gone, Marlene Dietrich, Lana Turner,
They have left that world one way or another.

Maybe this explains why, after all these years
Of marriage, mornings of casual undress, the naked nights,
All the scars and sags and blotches that create
An ever-broadening signature in the dark,
I still position myself to watch my wife
As she rises dripping from the bath, grabs a towel,
Then moves by the body's faithful memory
From drawer to drawer, from closet to mirror
And back, rejecting and selecting, posing
Like a woman who's entered a room of dazzled strangers,
Then retreating, as though surprised,
Then leaning in so close you think
She'll join her image in the glass.
Maybe this is why my son, age six, finds constant cause
To rush in upon us, breathless, ask a question –
Why the sky is blue all day and black all night –
Wait patiently for answers, only dimly realizing
What a privilege this really is,
This training ground for awe and separation.

How round and perfect the bodies were back then,
Before the troubles began. I had only
To stand on tiptoe to reach one, then another,
Like ripe apples on an overhanging branch,
To plunge my head between two swelling breasts.
I didn't, of course, not yet, anyway, though afterward,
In the echo chamber of the bathroom, before
The baby sitter came to see what I was up to, yes,
I rolled some lipstick on, put on my favorite dress,
Maybe some heels tonight, kissed the mirror,
Then intoned their names aloud,
First like a psalm, then like an elegy:
Florence, Muriel, Evelyn, Bebe, Ruth and Rose.

AUTHORITY

The boy can't remember shoplifting lately,
No doughnuts lately, no shiny fountain pens,
Or lying lately, either, or playing hooky,
Or sassing an adult or bullying a sissy.
He scans the room: bed made, jacket on the hook,
The white toy soldiers and the black
Toy soldiers and the leader
On his big roan horse on the just swept floor.
Nothing. Nothing he can think of. So why
Has his father summoned him into the parlor
In that voice like a holler down an empty barrel,
Where now he stands in place?
You're a bad kid, his father says, and slaps his face,
For nothing, *for good measure,*
This man who can see into his mind
Where the rat crouches in its usual corner
With its tongue tangled in its teeth.
Nothing? *Nothing. Liar! Thief!*

UNSPEAKABLE THINGS

He snatched the child skipping home from school
And in a park did unspeakable things.
Beyond the nature and the placement of the wounds,
Beyond the condition of the body bathed in leaves
Uncovered one year later in a depression
In the snow, we can't know what, although
The coroner's report is agonizingly acute.

In my lap, this fat book of serial murderers
I've been reading for three nights,
And wonder why, and keep reading, like
A summer's thriller on the beach.

Horror rises from each page like smog:
Sex with a doting uncle. . . cigarette scars
On ankle and thigh. . . the closet's close
Confining cellar darkness for a week
Until at one precise moment
Something like a flashbulb exploded in his head
And he prepared his pet mouse for slaughter.

Maybe from that pathetic spurting in his pants
As he strangled it, and maybe, afterwards,
As he stroked and stroked the mouse until
All the fur turned wet gray mush,
A ritual arose from unbearable
White heat you can almost imagine.

Then lost from sight for several years.
This, too, you can almost imagine, if you've known

Lost years in the indifferent city
In some apprenticeship in loneliness,
No girl, no job, no pals, though nobody died.

Probably he harbored his compulsion
In a dank hotel that caters to the lost
Who read their comic books and dream,
And, celibate, there honed his skills
With a knife and a rope, and the long and patient
Stalking and the erasures it must take
To become so different from one's kind. . . .

The mind lacks pockets for such horror,
Rank hatred and random desire
Stirred up in a gruesome stew
That made him not me, not you.

So what compelling force, when I finish, draws me
Out to the book store for one more?
By summer's end beside me stretches
An entire library shelf of death:
Closets, garages, sheds, wide fields of stubbled snow
We pass each day without notice;
The hammers, sour poisons, mutilations, viscera;
One confession, offered shyly, to a psychiatrist,
"It felt good."

When dredged up from muck to light, we find
The misspent, misfired molecules of. . . .What?

For a long time – months – I carried on my chain
A key I could not remember the door to.
It hung there, dancing its mysterious jangle,
Along with car key, office, and home,

Back door, side door, front, each of which I lock,
Then double back through all the rooms,
Wife, child, cat, then lock again, then sit down,
Then rise, peer out into the yard, then up,

And think of those prison gates surrounded by
The curious who wait for the lights to dim
Their long unnumbered moments, then flash back on as bright
As any new star in a black sky.

IMAGINATION

In the Holocaust survival literature, prisoners
Are constantly getting beaten up with clubs,
Getting smashed with clubs, battered, pounded, broken,
Until they're taught the lesson of the camps:
To be alive is punishable by death.
This happens everywhere, and at all times –
The testaments are vivid – but in all the stark photographs
I've never seen a picture of the clubs.

We have the pictures of the stiffened dead
In trenches, yes, but not the clubs
That put them there. We've seen the Lugers,
And those terrifying snarling Alsatian dogs,
And the whips, the hanging posts, the chimneys.

But not the clubs. Of course they were of hardwood,
The sort so dense that flesh is soft as fruit.
Forest ash? Birch? Oak, probably.

Since they also probably manufactured them, as Nazis
Manufactured all the grim necessities,
They must have been smooth and polished, like the canes
And crutches you see everywhere after a war –

Unless the clubs were mere local opportunities,
Foraged-after, fallen Polish branches
Unstripped of bark, craggy with knots.

And even as there was skin made into lamp shades
And hair for carpet slippers,

Perhaps the clubs were later carved
Into other useful items: toy shovels,
Pencils for the children, tiny Hummel figures,
Little disguised totem souvenirs

Of Jews and Gypsies, Politicals and Homosexuals,
And the SS might have traded in such things
Had they thought of them, after the war,
Though these were men of minuscule imagination
Given monstrous opportunity to wield it.

Totems, though. Yes. Carved folk figures
Of the dying and the dead. What better way to show
What they have done? Imagine,
The shelves of shops filled after the armistice,
Row after row for sale or show.

But the rougher clubs, the barky,
Knotty ones that did the most damage, that smashed
And maimed and murdered - kindling,
Probably, then ashes up the chimneys, wind-borne,
Then nothing but soft soot on the foreheads
Of the children as they trudged off to school -
The children, at their desks, hands folded.

ANDROGYNY

Just when you thought it safe enough
To enter the water clean as a knife, after the kids
Have been stuffed and quieted with picnic lunch
And bided the requisite hour
Building castles in the sand, there she is,

Or he is. It's a man.
Can't we all tell by the feet and hands
And the dark stubbling under the cheeks?

He's wearing a woman's fashionably snug
Two-piece bathing suit. His hair lush, curly, black,
Blooms over the shoulders, and further down, such breasts. . . .

All noise along the beach swells
Like a sudden wave, then stops.

To be both man and woman –
In all of us that potency, like a thousand
Messages into a thousand bottles
Returned, on the tides, with the answer. . . .

No. Rather, you imagine the late-night
Twisting conversations, and try to imagine
Sharp pain of depilation, weekly hormone shots,
And before the mirror the endless practice,

Like this, like that, like this.
And then the breasts, truly wondrous,
Bobbing in the air for all to see.

And then, of course, the knife. . . .

Two shapely, bathing-suited women grasp his arm
On either side. The three of them are laughing
Over something private. The grown-ups

Can't help themselves but stare. Two kids
Look down as the water takes away the sand,
Making moats of castles they've been playing in.

Then little Rebecca needs soothing,
And someone's sunburnt back needs creaming,
And a striped beach ball resumes its arc
Between that teenage boy and the other, *slap, slap,*

And the faint sound of derisive laughter,
And you in your simple singular flesh
Take off leaping toward the common water
Which cannot distinguish one sex from the other.

STOLEN KISSES: 1968

By midnight, thirty or forty people
Had gathered in the backyard and were dancing wildly
To a band that played a locally crazy mixture
Of blues and rock and roll
As though this were the world's
Last apocalyptic end-of-summer party.

I'd been married only several months,
And I don't know why I stood there by myself,
Leaning idly against the green truck,
Nor what brought the woman over to my side.
Night sky in the desert looms so large
Sky is all there is, and clouds drift past
Without margins. It was an eternal hot
And hopeless summer of the sort
Only the young survive, helpless in its grasp.

And the way the sudden deepening yellow
Of a jonquil bursting in a border bed
Could jam the brain's molecules so close
You want to start an argument,
Or quit your job, or buy a new convertible—
The way a passing *No* in conversation
Could end twenty years of marriage—
We took each other in our arms, and kissed.

A kiss by which one knows another
In a moment's breath, two histories
Entwining, and dissolving, and separating,
So you become at last yourself again.

Or do you? It was a kiss
So perfect I never went back.
The mouth is the place all loneliness begins.

I lay down on a hillside with a girl
Who had a waist like a wasp's
And a mouth like two pillows on the grass.

We kissed from after school
To after supper time, our mouths the kind of sore
The *penitentes* get

From walking on their knees, and wanting more.
Twice a week for several weeks
Until the first damp New England snow

Rushed down, and then we stopped –
We couldn't think where else to go!
I can almost call us back,

A boy with a boner and a girl as wet as spring,
Dry-humping in the grass,
The moans we must have made

Making room for tongues
Which in their endless wandering
Could have walked us to the next town.

In the years since, I've stood naked
In a hallway kissing a cold mirror,
And lain in bed kissing my own warm arm.

I've watched my son, the little reverie man,
Graze his lips with sensitive fingertips,
And suck his thumb until it drowned.

A woman said to me in anger once,
Kiss my Irish ass! And another
Kissed as though offering a multitude

Of tiny birds for supper.
A woman who kissed listlessly,
In boredom, in television light.

And my Cuban neighbor
Who kisses the air between our yards
To get her son's attention.

I've seen her in her doorway
Before the boyfriend comes
Gloss her lips in ancient invitation.

And once, in a whorehouse over a dance hall
In Jamaica, where under us steel drums
Matched beats with squeaky beds above,

I moved my mouth to hers.
Where else should sex begin!
My lips are not for business, she said.

Two faces are so close, so large,
You gaze into her eyes, believing you might see
Into the soul of another, that wordless puzzle of a place
Marked by lashes large as iron bars,

Flecked with color like the evening sky,
And in the center, as at the entrance
To a tunnel you're always about to enter,
The pupil looms, black and endless,
Broken only by a blink. Don't fool yourself.

Kissing isn't character. That woman in the yard
Beneath the Arizona stars
Kissed like everyone at once.
The mouth is the place all loneliness begins.

The anthropologist at the dinner party
Tells me the kiss directly on the mouth
Facilitated frontal intercourse,
And therefore intimacy, and therefore
(He goes on) the family itself. Surely, though,

Our ancestors must have known
A quick kiss beyond the fire's light
Could go as easily undetected
As a passing conversation, so the first kiss
Must also have facilitated the first betrayal.

If I were to steal a kiss tonight, at a party
Where I'd got too drunk to think,
Off in the guest bedroom with the coats,
The moral questions would line up like petitioners
Waiting for the church to open its huge doors.

Back then, maybe my wife stood
In another corner of the yard

Kissing another man,
And we were two sheets of glass
Mirroring each other
In our mutual but separate infidelities.

I've seen that far-flung woman in the years since, and,
In passing, there is no aura of seduction
Nor any standing uncomfortably about
Like guests at a cocktail party.
Though I noticed, the other day,
As we shook hands at the corner grocery
And traded scraps of parent-talk,
Her eyes held mine one moment longer
Than was necessary.

And I noticed, as I walked away, that she wore
A certain inexpensive, popular, powerful perfume
That always drowns my senses,
Drowns all memory, really, all moral sense, a scent
So strong it seemed like water rushing over me
So I stared wildly around
And didn't know what to say or do.

Back then, there was only sky, its local immensity,
And the two of us beneath it, kissing.
There were only the times, our mouths,

The turbulent long moment we were living in,
And the sad, loud, relentless music of the band.
The kiss was stolen, and consensual,
And singular. The kiss was a betrayal
And forbidden, therefore unforgettable.
The mouth is the place all loneliness begins.

THE MEANING OF ROMANCE

The baby's cranky and the night is hot.
First one breast then the other,
His mouth moving in a graspy snuffle

And before he knows just what he's got
He's fast asleep. My wife, adrift
In the darkened parlor on the couch

Oiling her dark and heavy breasts,
Her head lolling back and her socks off,
Asks me to tell the same old stories

That pulled us together when we were younger
Into a shared romance of our pasts.
We had a style of dancing Friday nights

We called the *Skinner Shuffle.*
Like a tango, or a bop, but slower,
Done together, in a stiff staccato meter

To the sweet and sensual *doo wop* of the day.
This in the Flats among the factories, 1957,
After spinning silk into cloth

All week in Skinner's Mills. *Do it,*
She says, so I get my comb and wet it
And return with my hair slicked back

Into a crest like a bold and silly bird
And my chest puffed up
Beneath my striped pajama top,

And suddenly we're gathered in the crowded, dark,
High-ceilinged rectangular dance hall
With all the Joes and Marys from the Projects,

All the Aces, Frenchys, Butchs,
All the Babs and Ruths and Dots.
Show me, she says. *Do it,*

So I rise from the couch
And she puts the records on, her dowry 45's,
Too-oo-oo-night, too-oo-night

More than any other ni-ight.
I pull her close, half-naked,
And we begin, my body canted

Slightly to the left, and hers straight on,
Me walking forward and her going back
And every three steps

A stop on a dime - a freeze, a stare -
Then a sort of rhythmic, wiggly shuffle,
And on around the parlor

Moving to the old tunes, the *doo-wops,*
And finally the fast one, *Hey, Bo Diddley,*
And I remove my pajama top, and she her bottom,

And here we are again doing the dirty boogie,
Crooning in our sweetest imitations
Of a capella baritone, a capella soprano

Ooly papa cow, papa cow, papa cow cow
Ooly papa cow, papa cow cow cow
I promise to remember The meaning of romance. . . .

The baby sleeps. The baby snores.
My wife shakes side to side, shoulders back,
Her blackened oiled nipples

Scattering drops of milk,
Then *bump bump,* two hips striking metal.
Ace, and Frenchy, Ruth, Dot,

Who made cloth from silk
Thirty years ago in Skinner's Mills,
What wonders are you spinning out,

What teenagers have you wrought,
Are you as proud and tough,
As silly and as sentimental,

Do you shine like oiled silk
And is the night as hot?

MR. & MRS. DEATH

Pretty soon I get up each morning and look
In the mirror: *You're going to die today.*
And pretty soon nothing has changed:
There I am filling the cup. There I am lifting
The fork to my mouth. And there's my father
In his eighties getting smaller,

And my mother whispering, *Your father*
Is deathly afraid of dying.
Is it the moment before the gasping in the doorway
He's worried about? Or the moment after?
There it is echoing down the long hallway
Going *argh argh* like the snake escaping the owl.
The woods are dark as ever there,
Among the oaks and berries, among the possible wolves.

In certain books I'm reading lately I hear
The poets saying, *I sat for hours*
Gazing at a yellow flower.
I confess my mind is not the sort of place
People wander through a Sunday park
Coaxing colors from the daffodils.
Rather, snatches of remembered conversations:
"A dog is not fallacious. . . ."
"I used to love my mother, 'til she died. . . ."

But it's not yet time for such recriminations.
It's only seven in the morning, and death
Shouldn't make us change everything.
Didn't I just make love with my wife,
And didn't I love it when I loved it?

As a child I used to hold each beloved person
In my mind, as in my hand. I thought:
If I drop them for a moment they will die.

And once, travelling the dark ribbon of highway
Through Ohio, I saw the lights of a town
Flickering, so many breathing souls,
Not one of them my father or a friend,
And felt relieved.

There were always two of me -
The boy climbing the elm and the boy
Waiting to catch me when I fell, the boy
In the mirror combing his defiant hair
And the boy watching. When I die
Won't the other go on watching: *There he is*
Rising from his easy chair, there he is
Clutching at his chest. . . .

That boy floats in white morning light.
His mouth is open wide. He wants to say
Sorry and he wants us to say,

Don't ever do that again, okay?
Isn't that all we want? To say
I'm sorry, Mr. Death, sorry, Mrs. Death.
Now won't you have some milk with me?

One morning I wanted it all to go away,
The haunting, repetitive, ever-flowering past.
And it did! So now I must make something up:
There's a mirror with somebody in it.
There's a mirror with nobody in it.

THE MAN IN THE BLACK TUXEDO

Every morning at precisely nine o'clock the undertaker
Waits for the light to change, tugs at his black bow tie,
Crosses the Boulevard Raspail and heads for the cafe
Where he stands at the bar drinking coffee with the other men,
Some with dirt-stained trousers and with hands
That could strangle a man in a minute,
And some in black suits with hands
That shake hands all day without tiring,
The grave digger, the embalmer, the wreath-maker,
Marble chipper, greeter, and chauffeur.

All of them are telling jokes
And laughing their raucous morning laughs
Which everyone in the cafe, including the elderly bartender
And the waitress with swollen feet and the dignified
Vietnamese cook take personally and look away,
Which is how it should be when undertakers laugh.

Except that today is his fiftieth birthday
And his fellow workers have brought these little joke gifts,
A carved woman *vanitas* grinning into a mirror,
And a miniature hooded executioner beside a miniature guillotine,
And a plastic flaccid penis, and a fake death certificate
With his name and his age and "Bonne Anniversaire"

And he has this new picture in his mind
That it will be him, not a stranger, lying face up
In the stone chapel of the Cemetery Montparnasse,
Him in his black tuxedo and his shiny shoes,
His face smoothed of its particulars.

This image fills his mind like water overflowing a cup,
As he straightens his jacket and tugs at his tie
And heads out into the rain
For the 8000th morning of his working life:

Today there will be six funerals, three in the morning
And three in the afternoon. He will assume the look
That is neither frown nor smile, and roll
His shoulders forward, and hold the huge black umbrella
A bit higher to accommodate
The tall weeping widow at the grave,
And pluck the dead petals
So the living petals will last at least another hour,
And stand up straight and hover behind
The gathered family like some forgotten mistress,

And now he imagines these are the jobs
He'll be assigned by the angels,
To be the general handler of the dead,
But one of them at last, chummy and familiar.
He will do everything the same, except his eyes
Will be sticky with embalming fluid
And his mouth will be sewn shut, as every morning

He will put the bodies into the earth
And every evening he will disinter them.
He will clean them and polish them
Like old shoes or tarnished silverware.

In heaven when they are stuttering their excuses
Or trying to make light
Of the new heaviness of their bodies
Or begging him to wipe the rain from their faces,

He will be the one to click the casket shut
And the one left to shiver in the rain.

What a way to go, he whispers, later,
Nodding to the setter to push the button
That will set the casket in its downward motion.
What a rotten day, he says to the Director
As they stand together
At six o'clock watching the last driver
Drive the last hearse down the slick road.

GOD'S MISTAKES

In the great city of Paris live all sorts of people,
Very tall Africans and very short,
Really tiny Europeans, grown-ups less than five feet tall.

And every morning on the Metro I see the man with the tumor
Ballooning from his neck, and the blind Tunisian flute-player.

And one Sunday, in the bone museum, at the Jardin des Plantes,
Among the dinosaurs and whales picked clean by time,
I saw the delicate, intertwined skeletons
Of fetal Siamese twins afloat in a bottle:

Marie et Christian, it says -
In Paris, they even baptize God's mistakes.

And outside the Pompidou,
There is the brash and balding mountain man
With the belly that could stop a train.
He earns his daily bread by playing the nasty fool
Before the crowds. How many people? 100? 200?

He yells, cajoles, and chases them;
Insults, humiliates, and captures them,
Then beats them on the head with an air-filled
Plastic bat or knees them in the crotch.

When he snatches an Asian tourist girl
And holds her like a trophy with one arm,
And with the other strips off his overalls

And stands before us in his billowing
Striped white and yellow boxer shorts, guffawing
At our discomfort and at hers, and points down,
Down there, beneath that huge belly,

We all gasp and we all clap,
Though we're pleased it isn't us.
He grabs her Nikon and stuffs it down
His shorts and snaps a snap. *Un souvenir,* he says.

But the belly itself, that's the freakish thing.
It sticks out from his body like an organ of its own,
Neither sagging like a beer belly nor round like a pregnancy,

But boxy, somehow, like a coffin for a baby,
Except there are these odd, protruding knots of muscle
Here and there, as if he built it up like that,

The way a man might idly squeeze a rubber ball
While watching television. As he jerks it up and down,
Like a puppet, like a Pierrot wooing his Pierrette,
It's like a brain case

Surrounding its own intelligence,
Its blind and foraging hunger and its wiles.

Hey, Africain, he yells, and mimes a few steps
Of a mincing queen. He points to a woman's breasts:
Pas beaucoup, he sneers. *Et vous!* he yells,

Pointing at me, and by now I am embarrassed
For the human race
That we all put up with this burlesque:

The leather-coated dwarf; the acned, tattooed German
Teenage punk with a symphony of earrings; the bald Italian
Who gets his head shined with a dirty cloth.

Still, I stand in my spot on the vast
And sloping apron of the Pompidou,
Grinning and embarrassed but pleased with the attention,

So when he summons me, I go to him,
Like a penitent to the altar,
Like a reluctant child to his father.

He lies down, very gingerly, on his back,
On a bed of nails, and commands,
Asseyez-vous sur moi!

So I sit, right on that thing, that belly.
He begins to move it, slowly, up and down,

And I am a child again in the park on a seesaw
The first time I could do it without help.
My mother is beaming and applauding, as is this crowd,
At my bad luck and my good nature, as I bounce

Up and down for all the world a fool to see,
Having a good old time, until the thing is done,
And I slide off, to go about my business

Of being a tourist in the great city of Paris
Among the albinos and the amputees, the retarded
And the refugees, the omnipresent unemployable

Winos and beggars, *Maries et Christians,* knowing for once
Exactly which one of God's mistakes I am.

CONFESSION

Forgive me, *Adonai*, Lord of the Jews,
God of my ancestors, Almighty *Yahweh, Elohim*
Who led Moses out of the wilderness,
But once as a teenager I gave my meek confession
At the Blessed Sacrament Church
So I might not feel so alone.
And now, at night, I cross myself again, yes,
Like any anxious mortal
In the confessional of the kitchen.
I kneel (also forbidden to the Jews)
Before the salt shakers, olive oil, sugar cubes,
I bruise my kneecaps bumping
Across the floor like a *penitente.*
I bow my head with my neck in the noose
As though to stare into my own casket,
And defer like the zebra to the lion, infidel to Allah,
And fold my hands in prayer
To any god who listens late at night,
And ask for absolution.

And thus begins the litany of the imperfect:
Adonai, forgive me, for I have neglected
To sniff the flowers like the lovers do.
I have never stared off into inanimate space
Like the apprentice mystics, for I have little spiritual life
And little intellectual life, for ideas weigh me down
Like heavy jewelry in the earlobes of a rich woman.
Forgive me, *Elohim,* for I've deadened the pain
With whiskey, with leers and laziness,
Pillage of the penis, pillage of the heart, etcetera, etcetera.

I won't tell any more. What good would it do?
At the end, I will stumble, like anyone,
Down Hillside Avenue, that long isthmus between earth and heaven,
With a few neighbors beside me, holding hands.
Some of those flowers I've forgotten to sniff –
A rose for love, a daffodil for humility –
I'll carry before me. I'll walk naked and fat,
With my slippers flapping and my beard grown long.

With every Jew, the good and the bad,
The great and small, with Judah Macabee
And my great-grandmother, Hashe Faige,
About whom many spoke and nobody praised,
With Esther Shapiro, Chaim Haberman, Sore Beyla,
I will lie down and sleep until the Judgement Day,
As it is written.
Will we comfort each other?
About this, the Talmud is silent.

However, here is my only son.
I offer him up, not like Abraham his Isaac,
Nor like Joseph his Jesus, but for consideration only.
He'll walk in my footsteps down Hillside Avenue,
Teetering, with his words spilling from his mouth,
With his sins cupped in one hand, good deeds in the other.
Only then, dear Lord, will you see
What sort of job I have done on this earth.

I WANT TO BE A GIRL

I am reading the paper every morning
And every morning the big sadnesses make their loud noises.
One hundred *X's* have suffocated
In the humid explosive gases of a chemical plant
And two hundred *Y's* were crushed in an earthquake
Because of three dishonest building inspectors.

After the great storm the sub-headline tells us
    Only Three People Drowned
I know, maybe a hundred human beings were at risk,
But still, to say "only" hurts everyone
Yet doesn't hurt enough to make us cry.

And then there are the back pages, where the little people live.
Maybe you knew them. I think, *maybe some tears there*
Because I know how important it is to be moved,
To be "cleansed by tears."

This morning, in the obituaries,
I see that one Mickie Rubinstein has died
"And is now shopping with her grandmother."

I see that Ima U. Eggman died
(These are facts), and around the breakfast table
We laughed more than we cried

Because maybe she developed a sense of humor
Like a stopped thermometer
Because some stupid parent decided to make a joke
That would last for nearly nine decades.

All my life I wanted to be with them when they died.
I say all my life, meaning when I was a little boy
I wanted to sit beside every dying human being
I had ever heard of –

The displaced Princess of Bohemia in her bed of a thousand
    flowers
And that drowning ten year old girl
In the mundane pissy waters of the YMCA swimming pool –

I wanted to hold their hands in mine
The way a child holds a piece of ice,
And watch the small soul melt from the body, and cry.

I knew, even then, there was nothing worse than death.

I know I have squandered a few tears at movies.
And once, on drugs, I wept
At the slow, painful birth of a yellow cactus flower.

I remember in sixth grade one day Joyce Mendelson
Suddenly broke into tears.
Nobody had died. I know for a fact
That nobody had insulted her that day
For her crossed eyes and chubby cheeks.

After school Miss Donoghue whispered to me:
"She's a girl and girls need no special reason to cry. . . ."

As a boy, I wanted to dog after the small sadnesses
Walking down Hillside Avenue.
I knew by their wringing hands and the slight erosion
Of sunlight around their bodies
That something terrible had happened.

I wanted to hold their hands,
And say, *there, there,* and maybe cry
A few small tears with them,
But I never did.

The barely pregnant acned teenage Helen Geoffrey
Abandoned by her boyfriend
And the immigrant Mrs. Ephros with the hairy upper lip
Who was just cheated at the corner grocery
And Arno Becher whose father used to slug him
For no reason he could think of. I know that my street
Was just as important as ancient Greece, and I know

They talked about themselves
In the dark, and pretty soon they were weeping,
Although nobody would read about it, nobody would cry.

Therefore, I want to be a girl,
Some Joyce Mendelson singing her inner overtures.

Therefore, I send my divining rod over the small earth of
my backyard.
But no sudden jerk of gravity pulls the branch down
Toward those rich and helpless waters.

"I want to be a girl," I tell my wife.
"You big silly," she says, cheerfully,

And pulls me so close I have no other place to go.
There was no reason for tears between us.

My wife is a wise woman.
When somebody dies, she skips the funeral
And writes them a personal letter

In perfectly slanted Palmer Method cursive script
And buries it in the backyard.

THE SHAPING GROUND

Outside, the snow is falling, falling.
She is reading a fat novel by the fire
And he is staring blankly into the flames
Like a man who hasn't found his feelings yet.
No unreachable itch yet,
No desire stirring in his pajama bottoms.

In her abundant novel about British country gentry life,
Foxes and hares, incest and frivolity,
The deepest winter of the 19th century, and so on,
The sexual event happens not spontaneously, but sideways,
With cunning, ambitious steps
From mansion to mansion across the countryside in snow.

In his wisdom, he knows that desire is sometimes as far away
As Wednesday is from Saturday,
As far away as Beijing from Istanbul by train,
Northwards on the old trade route through Siberia
Where cold is so cold you barely mention it,
You're only passing through.

The snow is falling like infinite particulars
Before they hit the blurring ground.
What would it take, she wonders, to get him going?
Some small act of generosity?
She takes his empty tea cup down the corridor

To the sink, washes it, rinses it, dries it,
Puts it in the cabinet. He makes a reasonable mistake
In idle conversation, some mis-memory

About their honeymoon in 1968,
And he apologizes, and she says, "That's okay,"
And doesn't go on to say, *Everyone makes a mistake. . . .*

Suddenly, he looks up from the blazing fire
And says something he's never said before,
Never even thought before: "Honey," he says,
"Have you ever taken Jesus into your heart?"

And she turns down the corner of the page,
Right at the point where the shamed, repentant
Forgiven brother and sister decide
To go at it again, to repeat their error endlessly,
To sire generations of mindless blond children,
And the words are starting to burn up
On the page, right then, the wife, this prisoner
Of the common groove and the common room,

This female anima of all the moods
Of many years of marriage, she says, like the hungry drunk
To the Salvation Army chaplain,
Like the soldier crushed in honest defeat
To his enemy, she says to her husband,
Like an unhorsed rider to the horse,
Like the wise victim of a common scam,

Like the present tense to the past tense,
Like the anthem to the flagpole,
The explosion to the ammunition,
"Yes, I will take Jesus into my heart.
In my heart, there's room for everyone!"

And they both laugh, knowing that
The distance between the parlor and the bedroom

Is the distance between tragedy and comedy,
Between the words of the spell
And the magic event, miles and miles
Of household corridors in which whole lives
Are lived, knowing that this will be
The arduous trek between habit and passion.
Snow is falling, falling on the shaping ground.

GENEALOGY

Like a face in a swirling crowd you almost recognize,
Almost can find the name for,
Like the face of your father barely visible in dreams
And calling out something like your name,

Like the face of your young son
At the table, bent over his fork and spoon,
His features changing before your eyes,

And the face confronted in the morning mirror
That hints at who you are on this particular day,
And the face in the family album
That hints at who you were on that particular day
Gathered with the other faces, cousins, aunts, grandparents
Around a picnic table, Forest Park, 1948,

And behind them, between them, those old friends,
Just hanging around, pecking like wingless birds
Unable to leave, the ancestors –
He who died with his seeds
Stuck like burrs in his pockets,
And his brother who spread his seed like a drunken farmer
And out came Mendel ben Horse-Trader,
Moishe Fisherman, Bella the Seamstress,

And out came one outright Velvel the Crook
And his daughter who drowned herself
In the filthy waters of the third-level canal,
Holyoke, Massachusetts, June, 1927. . . .

And after the names, the mysterious question arises
About the parcelling out of character
Like shavings from a great big chunk of wood

Some blind carpenter seems always to be turning on his lathe:
Which qualities lost and which gained,
Which might lie hidden in its infinite thicket.

I'd love to float down the long rivers of Canaan
That lead to Adam and Eve in the Garden
And ask question after personal question –

Which one among you chose that lucky path
And how you felt inside, getting up that fateful morning,
What words you spoke first thing,
What lunch you packed, which horse to saddle up?

And then of course, which ancestral talmudist,
Gnawing at the given words,
Which flatulent diarist, which absent-minded thief,

Which *Chaim Yankel* daydreaming behind his horse and plow,
Which *cheder* boy lost in his yawning
Prayers for rising and for washing up,

Could possibly have survived
The urgent, dire, present tense –

No cabbage on the table, pogrom outside the door,
Plague leaping house to house causing the constant
Nomadic expulsions of the medieval Jews –

Could possibly have survived
While thinking of something else?

Isn't that an *Orlen,* the man or the woman
Always thinking of something else?

Like how that Cossack rifle
Is like a flower sticking up
From a rare enamel lavender vase, then *boom!*
You're dead. And that word "vase" must come from

The Latin for *vas* which means vessel,
And vessels are also ships for going as far
Away as one can get from here to there.

Then *boom!* you find yourself on another shore
With shoes that don't fit and a language
Dead for twenty centuries. Isn't it useless,
This looking back and counting up
Who begat whom begat whom?

We can never truly know those dead progenitors,
Can never unearth the census of the selves,
Moment blending into moment, the consummate angels
And the failed angels vying for attention,

Or in which language they chose to learn
The words for "Mister" "What" or "Sorry"
Or what wherewithal, which tools to bring,
And which night to run and which night to make love
And which sperm of millions courted which egg, and won,

Until that morning my son
Bent down and rose up
With a horseshoe and a bent nail dangling from his fist!

Steve Orlen was born and raised on Hillside Avenue in Holyoke, Massachusetts. His previous books of poetry include *Permission to Speak, A Place at the Table,* and *The Bridge of Sighs.* He teaches in the Creative Writing Program at the University of Arizona in Tucson, and in the low-residency MFA Program at Warren Wilson College.

Orlen is a wonderful poet and one of the best practitioners of free verse writing today. The sounds of his poems bang and glide. Most fine poetry strikes the mind and heart. This is true of Orlen as well, but his poems also strike the ear. They feel good in the mouth.

—Stephen Dobyns

Orlen's *Bridge of Sighs*, like Eliot's "Prufrock," is filled with many human voices, but they are the voices around us, the recognizable voices of people we know too well.... He builds from memory, from old photographs, mental snapshots of the past, and he knows where to break a line and also how to break your heart.

— Mark Hillringhouse
in *The Literary Review*

Cover Illustration by: Gail Marcus Orlen
Cover Design by: Kimberly Snow Logsdon

$11.95

ISBN 1-881163-23-7

Miami University Press
Oxford, Ohio

THE *New* SMART

HOW NURTURING CREATIVITY
WILL HELP CHILDREN THRIVE

TERRY ROBERTS, PhD
FOREWORD BY HOWARD GARDNER